BRIT

by John Dudley

LONDON

Ian Allan Ltd

RALLYING
to
Monte
Carlo

by Mike Couper

with foreword by
Raymond Baxter

Le Rallye is one of the greatest annual motoring events to arouse the sporting spirit of people throughout the world. And there can be no more enthusiastic a participant than Mike Couper, who has driven many different makes of British cars to Monte Carlo in every Rally since 1939. This first-hand account of his many journeyings across the snow-bound continent with its many hazards and heartbreaks, will thrill everyone interested in motor sport.

208 pp. ; 16 pp. illustrations. 3 colour plates. Route Maps. 8½ ins. x 5½ ins. Fully bound.

16/-

published by

Ian Allan Ltd

HAMPTON COURT, SURREY

Contents

Introduction

O NCE again a new edition of the *A.B.C. of British Cars* surveys the numerous products of the British motor industry. Most of the popular makes are continued with only minor changes this year, but there have been a number of interesting additions, mostly in the medium size range. For instance, Jaguar have introduced the 2·4-litre saloon, Armstrong–Siddeley have two new 2·3-litre models and the Rootes Group have produced a brand new Sunbeam—the 1¼-litre Rapier saloon.

The long list of 100 m.p.h. British cars continues to grow. The 4-cylinder Armstrong–Siddeley Sapphire, the 2·4-litre Jaguar, the One-o-Four series of Daimlers, the Gran Turismo Alvis, and the new Bentley and Rolls-Royce models are all capable of passing the magic figure. There are several new British sports cars, too. These include the Series A M.G.—a good example of the use of motor racing improving the breed—the T.R.3 version of the Triumph, the Austin Healey M, and the cheap Morgan 4/4 Series II.

Among the popular makes Standard have introduced a new version of the well-known Vanguard saloon which has been one of Britain's most successful post-war family motor cars. The extensive Ford range includes two new estate cars—the Escort and the Squire—based on the successful Anglia and Prefect 10-h.p. saloons.

Technical advances have not been neglected. The big Sapphire saloons are now offered with controlled power steering, and power-operated windows. The automatic gearbox is now available on the Austin Princess. Tubeless tyres are gradually being introduced. This year Singer have become the first British firm to take the step of offering a car equipped with tubeless tyres and without a spare wheel. More models are available with overdrive either as an optional extra, or—as in the case of the new Sunbeam—as a standard feature.

In this new edition quick reference panels have been included so that the salient features of each car can be spotted at a glance. Each new model (i.e. those not mentioned in the 1955 *A.B.C. of British Cars*) is marked with an asterisk.

Fuel consumption figures and maximum speeds are approximate.

JOHN DUDLEY.

A.C.

A.C. Cars, Ltd.,

Thames Ditton,

Surrey.

- ACE & ACECA: 100 m.p.h.+, 2-litre, 6-cyl., o.h.c. engine, 3 S.U. carbs., 4-speed synchromesh gearbox with central lever. Transverse leaf springs and wishbones front and rear. Girling hydraulic brakes and Al-Fin drums. Wire wheels. ACE 2-door, 2-seater sports. ACECA 2-door, 2-seater sports saloon.

- A.C. SALOON: 80 m.p.h., 2-litre, 6-cyl. o.h.c. engine, 3 S.U. carbs., 4-speed synchromesh gearbox with central lever. Half-elliptic suspension to all four wheels. Girling hydraulic brakes. 2-door or 4-door, 4-seater saloons.

THE A.C. Ace sports car, with the coupé version—the Aceca—has already won its spurs in rallies and sports car races, and is proving a popular car with enthusiasts. Powered by the 2-litre 6-cylinder engine, the Ace has a dry weight of only 1,685 lb. This gives a very favourable power-weight ratio and permits speeds of over 100 m.p.h. and very rapid acceleration. Suspension all round is by transverse leaf and wishbones. A fuel consumption of 26 m.p.g. is claimed.

The Thames Ditton factory is now concentrating on production of these two models, but the 2-litre A.C. saloon is still available in 2-door and 4-door form. This car has half elliptic suspension to all four wheels—an unusual feature in these days of almost universal independent front suspension.

Specifications

Model	c.c.	No. of Cyls.	Max. B.H.P.	Wheel Base	Max. Track	Length	Width	Turning Circle
ACE & ACECA	1,991	6	90	7′ 6″	4′ 2″	12′ 7½″	4′ 11½″	36′ 5″
SALOON ...	1,991	6	76	9′ 9″	4′ 8″	15′ 4″	5′ 7″	40′

Total U.K. Prices

ACE ..	.. ..	£1,651 3s. 0d.
ACECA	.. ..	£2,063 17s. 0d.
TWO-DOOR SALOON	.. .. ..	£1,542 15s. 8d.
FOUR-DOOR SALOON	.. .. ..	£1,663 4s. 1d.

Facing page—Top : A.C. Aceca ; Centre : A.C. 2-litre, 2-door Saloon ; Bottom : A.C. Ace

Allard

Allard Motor Co., Ltd.,

24-28, High Street,

Clapham, S.W.4.

- MONTE CARLO AND SAFARI: 100 m.p.h., 6-cyl., 3½-litre, o.h.v. Jaguar engine with 4-speed synchromesh gearbox, or 5½-litre V.8-cyl. Cadillac engine with fluid drive and hydramatic transmission. Monte Carlo, 5/6-seater, 4-door coachbuilt saloon, Safari, 6-seater coachbuilt estate car.

- K.3 TOURER: Same choice of engines and transmission. 3-seater, 2-door touring body with fabric hood and wind-up windows.

- J.2R COMPETITION: 100 m.p.h. V.8-cyl., 5½-litre Cadillac engine with 4 carbs., 3-speed manual gearbox. Coil spring i.f.s. De Dion rear axle. 2-seater, 2-door sports body.

FOUR models are offered in the Allard range for 1956. Three of these—the Monte Carlo saloon, the Safari estate car, and the K.3 Tourer—have the choice of the 3½-litre, 6-cylinder Jaguar engine (fitted in Allards for the first time this year) or the 5½-litre Cadillac power unit. The fourth model—the J.2R Competition version—has the Cadillac engine. When the Jaguar engine is used, a normal 4-speed synchromesh gearbox is fitted. With the Cadillac engine there is a fluid drive and Hydramatic transmission, although the competition car has a 3-speed manual gearbox.

The Monte Carlo is a five-six-seater aluminium panelled coachbuilt saloon mounted on a tubular chassis with a divided front

Allard Safari Estate Car

Allard Monte Carlo Saloon

axle, De Dion rear axle, and coil springs front and rear. This model and the Safari may be recognized by the " A " shaped radiator. The K.3 has a similar chassis, but a different body and a smaller petrol tank. The J.2R has a rather high ground clearance and a small oblong radiator opening. The Palm Beach model, which was available last year with a choice of Consul or Zephyr engines, is discontinued.

Specifications

Model	c.c.	No. of Cyls.	Max. B.H.P.	Wheel Base	Max. Track	Length	Width	Turning Circle
MONTE CARLO	3,442	6 or V.8	190	9′ 4″	4′ 10½″	16′	5′ 11″	40′
SAFARI... K.3 ...	5,420		250	8′ 4″	4′ 10½″	14′ 9″	5′ 6″	38′
J.2.R	5,420	V.8	270	8′	4′ 3″	12′ 6″	4′ 11″	—

Total U.K. Prices

MONTE CARLO SALOON	..	..	..	..	£2,674 7s. 0d.
SAFARI ESTATE CAR	..	..	..	..	£2,674 7s. 0d.
J.2R	..	..	..	..	£2,584 7s. 0d.
K.3	..	..	..	..	£2,306 17s. 0d.

9

Alvis

**Alvis Ltd.,
Holyhead Road,
Coventry.**

● GRAN TURISMO:* 100 m.p.h.+, 6-cyl., 3-litre o.h.v. engine. Twin S.U. carbs. 4-speed synchromesh gearbox with central lever. Coil spring and wishbone i.f.s. Wire wheels. 2-door, 4-seater sports saloon by Graber of Berne.

THE latest version of the Alvis 3-litre series is the TC108/G 3-litre sports saloon—the Gran Turismo—with coachwork by the Swiss f.r.m of Graber. This has a neat all-enveloping body with a square, slightly pointed, radiator grille carrying the usual Alvis triangle nameplate. Visibility is excellent with a " wraparound " rear window and narrow pillars. The Dunlop wire

Alvis Gran Turismo

wheels have " knock off " hub caps, and there is a large luggage compartment with a separate spare wheel container.

The Grey Lady and the drophead model of previous years are now discontinued. Development work on a completely new Alvis is said to be continuing.

The Alvis is a high performance car with a top speed of over 100 m.p.h.

Specifications

Model	c.c.	No. of Cyls.	Max. B.H.P.	Wheel Base	Max. Track	Length	Width	Turning Circle
GRAN TURISMO	2,993	6	104	9′ 3½″	4′ 6⅝″	15′ 2½″	5′ 6″	39′ 6″

Total U.K. Prices

T.C. 108/G GRAN TURISMO .. .. .. £2,776 7s. 0d.

Armstrong Siddeley

Armstrong-Siddeley

Motors Ltd.,

Parkside,

Coventry.

- SAPPHIRE MODEL 234*: 100 m.p.h.+. 4-cyl., 2·3-litre o.h.v. engine. Twin S.U. carbs., 4-speed synchromesh gearbox with hydraulic clutch, central control and optional overdrive. Coil spring and wishbone i.f.s. Heater and windscreen washers fitted. 4-door, 4-light, 4/5-seater saloon.

- MODEL 236*: 90 m.p.h.+, 6-cyl., 2·3-litre o.h.v. engine. Single Stromberg carb. 4-speed synchromesh gearbox with manumatic no clutch gear change. Central control. Optional overdrive. Other details the same as Model 234.

- MODEL 346: 100 m.p.h.+, 6-cyl., 3½-litre o.h.v. engine. Twin carbs. or single carb. 4-speed synchromesh gearbox with steering column control, 4-speed electric preselector box, or 4-speed automatic gearbox. Overdrive optional. Coil spring and wishbone i.f.s. Optional controlled power steering. Optional adjustable ride control, and power operated windows. Fitted heater. 4-door, 6-light, 5/6-seater saloon or limousine.

TWO noteworthy additions to the Armstrong–Siddeley range for 1956 are the Sapphire Model 234 and 236 saloons. The 234 is a high performance saloon with a 4-cylinder, 2·3-litre engine and a top speed of over 100 m.p.h. Overdrive is an optional extra and a favourable fuel consumption of 30 m.p.g. is

Above : Armstrong Siddeley Sapphire

Left : Controls of the Sapphire 236

Below : Armstrong Siddeley 234

claimed. There is a normal 4-speed synchromesh gearbox, and standard equipment includes a heater and demister, windscreen washers, and lights in the boot and under the bonnet. The 236 has a 6-cylinder, 2·3-litre engine with a lower performance and Manumatic no-clutch pedal gear change. Otherwise the specifications are similar.

These two new models join the already well-established Sapphire 346 models which have a 3½-litre, 6-cylinder engine. With twin Stromberg carburettors—an optional extra—the big Sapphire is a 100 m.p.h. car. Overdrive is optional, and there is a choice of automatic, electric preselector or synchromesh gearbox. Optional extras this year include controlled power steering, and adjustable ride control—a system by which the rear dampers can be adjusted from the instrument panel. Power-operated windows are also available. Saloon and Limousine models are made. The Sapphire models all have the Armstrong-Siddeley pointed radiator with its vertical grille and sphinx mascot.

Specifications

Model	c.c.	No. of Cyls.	Max. B.H.P.	Wheel Base	Max. Track	Length	Width	Turning Circle
234	2,290	4	120	9' 3"	4' 7⅛"	15'	5' 8½"	39' 8"
236	2,309	6	85	9' 3"	4' 7"	15'	5' 8"	39' 8"
346 SALOON ...	3,435	6	125 or 150	9' 6"	4' 9½"	16' 1"	6'	42' 6"
346 LIMOUSINE	3,435	6	125 or 150	11' 1"	4' 9½"	17' 8"	6'	45'

Total U.K. Prices

SAPPHIRE 234	£1,599 17s. 0d.
SAPPHIRE 236	£1,657 7s. 0d.
SAPPHIRE 346 SALOON (Automatic)	£2,107 7s. 0d.
SAPPHIRE 346 LIMOUSINE (Preselective) ..	£2,866 7s. 0d.
SAPPHIRE 346 SALOON (S/M)	£1,823 17s. 0d.
SAPPHIRE 346 SALOON (Preselective)	£1,928 17s. 0d.

Aston Martin

**Aston Martin Ltd.,
Feltham,
Middlesex.**

- D.B. 2-4: 100 m.p.h.+, 6-cyl., twin o.h.c., 3-litre engine. (Competition head optional.) 4-speed synchromesh gearbox with central control. Fitted heater and air-conditioning. 2-door, 2/4-seater sports saloon, hardtop* or drophead coupé.

A NEW hardtop version of the famous Aston Martin D.B.2-4 sports saloon is available this year. The D.B.2-4 is a two-seater but has additional seats for children or occasional adult passengers and a roomy luggage compartment. The power unit is the 3-litre twin o.h.c. 6-cylinder engine which is used with such outstanding success in the Aston Martin sports racing machines. This is served by twin variable jet carburettors. A competition type head with larger inlet and exhaust valves and high lift cam-shafts is an optional extra for those who are interested in using

their D.B.2-4 for competition work. The sports saloon has a "Four" light body with a stubby tail. The big rear window is actually in the boot door and opens with it. The new hardtop has smaller windows at the rear, and a jutting boot. The square radiator has a horizontal grille and is surmounted by the winged Aston Martin badge. New features on all the D.B.2-4s this year are air-conditioning to the body through the central aperture in the bonnet, a fly-off handbrake at the side of the gear lever, a new rear axle, and a concealed petrol filler cap in the rear wing which is operated by remote control from inside the car. The competition two-seater, D.B.3.S, is also on sale to the public.

Above : Aston Martin DB2-4 Mk. II Drophead Coupé
Left : Aston Martin DB2-4 Hardtop
Below : Aston Martin DB2-4 Mk. II Sports Saloon

Specifications

Model	c.c.	No. of Cyls.	Max. B.H.P.	Wheel Base	Max. Track	Length	Width	Turning Circle
D.B.2–4...	2,922	6	140	8' 3"	4' 6"	14' 3½"	5' 5"	35'
D.B.3.S ...	2,922	6	210	7' 3"	4' 4"	12' 10"	5' 2"	30'

Total U.K. Prices

D.B. 2–4 Mk. II Hardtop	.. .. ..	£3,076	7s. 0d.
D.B. 2–4 Mk. II Saloon..	.. .. ..	£3,076	7s. 0d.
D.B. 2–4 Mk. II Drophead	.. .. ..	£3,301	7s. 0d.
D.B.–3.S. Competition ..	.. .. ..	£3,901	7s. 0d.

Austin

Austin Motor Co., Ltd., Longbridge, Birmingham.

- SEVEN: 60 m.p.h.+, 4-cyl., 800 c.c. o.h.v. engine; 4-speed gearbox with central control lever. Coil spring and wishbone i.f.s. 2-or 4-door saloons.

- CAMBRIDGE: 80 m.p.h.+, 4-cyl., 1½-litre o.h.v. engine, or 70 m.p.h., +4-cyl. 1¼-litre o.h.v. engine. 4-speed gearbox with steering column control. Tubeless tyres and sliding head now available; 4-door, 4-seater saloon.

- WESTMINSTER: 90 m.p.h.+, 6-cyl., 2½-litre o.h.v. engine. 4-speed gearbox with steering column control. Overdrive optional. Tubeless tyres, coil spring i.f.s., 4-door, 4/5 seater saloon.

- PRINCESS: 90 m.p.h.+, 6-cyl., 4-litre, o.h.v. engine. 4-speed gearbox with steering column change. Automatic box optional, Coil spring i.f.s., 4-door, 6-seater saloon. Limousine L.W.B. saloons or L.W.B. limousine.

THE popular baby of the Austin range, the A.30 Seven, is the descendant of a famous line of small cars and it certainly lives up to its tradition. Powered by a lively overhead valve engine which gives a maximum road speed of about 67 m.p.h., it can claim a fuel consumption of 54 m.p.g. at a steady 30 m.p.h. The full width body has inbuilt headlights but separate side lights mounted well back on top of the front wings. The usual winged " A " mascot is mounted on the bonnet. A 4-door and a 2-door model are available. Optional equipment includes over-riders, ashtrays, opening rear windows (on the 2-door model), heater and radio. A Countryman estate car version is also available.

Austin Princess

The Cambridge models are continued with only minor changes for 1956. These changes include separate locking filler caps, winding windows, wider front seat adjustment, and a new type of flashing indicator designed to avoid confusion with other lights. Tubeless tyres are being introduced gradually, and a small proportion of models is now being fitted with a sliding head. The A.40 and A.50 versions are identical in appearance, but the A.50 has a slightly larger engine. Both engines are of British Motor Corporation design. There is a wide closely grilled radiator

Austin A.90 " Six " Westminster

Austin A.40–A.50 Cambridge

opening and a wide chromium edged air scoop at the front of the bonnet. The A.40 is available in 2-door or 4-door form and there is a standard and a de-luxe version of each. The A.50 is only available as a 4-door, but there is a standard and a de-luxe version.

Austin A.30 " Seven " Saloon

Top speed is about 79 m.p.h. Fuel consumption at 30 m.p.h. is 43 m.p.g., and at high speeds 28 m.p.g.

The 90 m.p.h. 6-cylinder Westminster, is offered this year with overdrive—providing two extra driving ratios—as an optional feature. In appearance it is very much the big brother of the Cambridge, but it has chromium flashes on the sides of the body. Overall fuel consumption is claimed to be 22 m.p.g. The standard model has P.V.C. coated fabric seat trimmings, and the heater, radio, and electric clock are optional extras. The de-luxe model has seats faced with hide, a heater and various other extras as standard.

The largest of the Austin range is the 6-cylinder Princess, available in saloon or limousine form. This year it is offered with an automatic gearbox. The 4-litre A.135 engine gives a top speed of nearly 90 m.p.h. with a fuel consumption range of 15 to 17 m.p.g. The radiator is slightly pointed with a vertical grille, and has the Austin wheel badge at the top. Deep valances cover the rear wheels. The long wheelbase saloons and limousine now have tubeless tyres.

Specifications

Model	*c.c.*	*No. of Cyls.*	*Max. B.H.P.*	*Wheel Base*	*Max. Track*	*Length*	*Width*	*Turning Circle*
A.30	800	4	28	6′ 7½″	3′ 9¼″	11′ 4⅜″	4′ 7⅛″	35′
A.40	1,200	4	42	8′ 3¼″	4′ 1″	13′ 6½″	5′ 1½″	36′
A.50	1,489	4	50	8′ 3¼″	4′ 1″	13′ 6½″	5′ 1½″	36′
A.90	2,639	6	85	8′ 7¾″	4′ 3½″	14′ 2¼″	5′ 4″	36′
A.135 SALOON	3,995	6	—	9′ 11¼″	5′	16′ 1½″	6′ 1″	43′
A.135 LWB LIMOUSINE ..	3,995	6	—	11′	5′	17′ 11″	6′ 1″	45′ 6″

Total U.K. Prices

A.30 Two-Door Saloon	£503 17s. 0d.
A.30 Four-door Saloon	£533 17s. 0d.
A.30 Countryman	£593 17s. 0d.
A.40 Two-door Saloon	£703 7s. 0d.
A.40 Four-door Saloon	£748 7s. 0d.
A.40 Countryman	£775 7s. 0d.
A.50 Four-door Saloon	£718 7s. 0d.
A.90 Saloon	£838 7s. 0d.
A.135 Saloon	£2,498 17s. 0d.
A.135 Touring Limousine	£2,573 17s. 0d.
A.135 L.W.B. Saloon	£3,001 7s. 0d.
A.135 L.W.B. Touring Limousine	£3,001 7s. 0d.

Austin Healey

Donald Healey Motor
Co., Ltd.,

The Cape,
Warwick.

- HUNDRED: 100 m.p.h.+, 4-cyl., 2½-litre o.h.v. engine. 4-speed synchromesh gearbox with overdrive. Central change control. Coil spring i.f.s. with torsion bar. 2-door sports. Detachable hardtop available.

- HUNDRED M* With racing modifications, high compression pistons, louvred bonnet, etc.

THIS fine British sports car, manufactured by the Donald Healey Company and distributed throughout the world by Austin agents, has a top speed of over 110 m.p.h. It is not very long ago that a streamlined version achieved 192·7 m.p.h. in the United States. The 2½-litre, 4-cylinder engine is served by twin S.U. carburettors. Overdrive—a standard fitting—combined with the new 4-speed synchromesh gearbox gives, in effect, six forward speeds. Full weather protection includes a folding windshield, and a disappearing hood. New this year is the Hundred M. built for competition work. This may be recognized externally by the louvred bonnet top, the leather bonnet strap, and the two-tone

Austin Healey " Hundred "

20

Austin Healey " Hundred M "

finish. This model has high compression pistons, a high lift cam-shaft, special inlet manifolds, racing suspension and other modifications.

Specifications

Model	c.c.	No. of Cyls.	Max. B.H.P.	Wheel Base	Max. Track	Length	Width	Turning Circle
HUNDRED ...	2,660	4	90	7' 6"	4' 2¾"	12' 7½"	5' 0½"	35'
HUNDRED M...	2,660	4	110	7' 6"	4' 2¾"	12' 7½"	5' 0½"	35'

Total U.K. Prices

HUNDRED 2-SEATER   ..   ..   £1,226   7s.   0d.

Bentley

Bentley Motors (1931)

Ltd.,

14-15, Conduit Street,

London, W.1.

- S. SERIES:* 100 m.p.h.+, 6-cyl., 4·9-litre engine. Automatic gearbox. Servo-assisted brakes. Fitted heater and demister. 5/6-seater, 4-door saloon.

- CONTINENTAL: 100 m.p.h.+, 6-cyl., 4·9-litre engine. Automatic gearbox. Servo-assisted brakes. Fitted heater and demister. Drophead coupé and 2-door Sports saloon.

THE new Series S Bentley is the sister car of the Rolls–Royce Silver Cloud and, of course, it comes from the same factory. For the first time in the Series S and the Silver Cloud, the firm offer identical cars in the two makes. The radiator is the only difference. The Series S has the famous slightly pointed Bentley radiator. The powerful 6-cylinder engine has twin S.U. car-

Front seat of Bentley "S" series

burettors and a 4-port cylinder head instead of a 6-port cylinder head as on previous Bentleys.

The Bentley Continental sports models are brought into line with the new Series S this year, and have the new engine. Their special lightweight all-metal bodies give them a remarkable power-

Bentley Continental Sports Saloon

Bentley Continental Drophead Coupé

Bentley " S " series four-door Saloon

weight ratio. Three models are available—the Drophead Coupé and Sports Saloon by Park Ward and the Mulliner Sports Saloon. The Mulliner sports saloon, it will be noticed, has fin-like rear mudguards to stabilize the car at high speeds. The front seats have folding armrests and their squabs are adjustable for rake in three positions.

On all Bentleys independent front suspension is by coil springs with hydraulic shock dampers and anti-roll rod, while at the rear suspension is by semi-elliptic leaf springs with hydraulic shock dampers and Z type anti-roll bar.

Specifications

Model	c.c.	No. of Cyls.	Max. B.H.P.	Wheel Base	Max. Track	Length	Width	Turning Circle
SERIES S ...	4,887	6	—	10' 3"	5'	17' 8"	6' 2¾"	41' 8"
CONTINENTAL	4,887	6	—	10' 3"	5'	17' 6"	5' 11½"	41' 8"

Total U.K. Prices

SERIES S SALOON	£4,943 17s. 0d.
CONTINENTAL MULLINER SPORTS SALOON ..	£7,441 7s. 0d.
CONTINENTAL PARK WARD SPORTS SALOON ..	£7,163 17s. 0d.
CONTINENTAL PARK WARD DROPHEAD COUPÉ ..	£7,163 17s. 0d.

Bristol

**The Motor Division,
Bristol Aeroplane Co.,
Ltd.,**

**Filton,
Bristol.**

● BRISTOL 405: 100 m.p.h.+, 6-cyl., o.h.v., 2-litre engine. 4-speed synchromesh gearbox (free-wheel in-built into first speed). Central control. Overdrive. Wishbone and transverse spring i.f.s. Heater-demister. 4-seater, 4-door saloon, or 2-door drophead coupé.

FOR 1956 the Bristol range will consist of two models—the 405 4-door saloon, and the 405 2-door drophead coupé. Both are continued with only minor changes from 1955. The bumpers now carry over-riders and, as an additional passenger safety measure, the parcel shelf facing the front passenger seat is trimmed with leather-covered sorbo rubber. Note the neat square radiator duct, the humped air scoop on top of the bonnet and the typical Bristol wheels, pierced for brake ventilation. The engine is the 100.B overhead valve 6-cylinder, 2-litre with an R.A.C. rating

Bristol 405 Saloon

of 16·2 h.p. This puts the car in the 100 m.p.h. class and gives it a high cruising speed, combined with economical fuel consumption. The makers claim the consumption at 80 m.p.h. to be 20 m.p.g., and at 60 m.p.h., 24 m.p.g. Overdrive is provided with an automatic switch which ensures a return to direct fourth gear after a lower gear has been engaged. Flashing turn indicators operated by a time switch are incorporated with the side lamps. A long range spot lamp is situated in the radiator duct. Fitted portmanteaux are available in the spacious luggage boot as an optional extra. Twin interior lights are fitted in the saloon—one on each

Bristol 405 Drophead

central door pillar. Independent front suspension is by wishbone arms and a transverse multi-leaf spring. Rear suspension is by torsion bars running fore and aft. Large hydraulic double acting telescopic shock absorbers are fitted at front and rear. The Bristol is a fine sports tourer of aerodynamic design and its powerful engine has been well tried in competition work.

Specifications

Model	c.c.	No. of Cyls.	Max. B.H.P.	Wheel Base	Max. Track	Length	Width	Turning Circle
405	1,971	6	105	9' 6"	4' 6"	15' 9¼"	5' 8"	37' 6"

Total U.K. Prices

BRISTOL 405 FOUR-DOOR SALOON	.. ..	£3,586 7s. 0d.
BRISTOL 405 DROPHEAD COUPÉ ..	.. ..	£3,676 7s. 0d.

Daimler

The Daimler Co., Ltd.,

Radford Works,

Coventry.

- CONQUEST: 80 m.p.h.+, 6-cyl., 2½-litre o.h.v. engine; 4-speed preselector gearbox. Steering column control. Fluid transmission. Coil sp ing i.f.s. Heater fitted. 4-door, 5-seater saloon.

- CONQUEST CENTURY: 90 m.p.h.+, 6-cyl., 2½-litre o.h.v. engine with twin carbs. Other details as for Conquest, but there is also the 2/3-seater CONQUEST DROPHEAD COUPÉ* with the Century engine.

- ONE-O-FOUR:* 100 m.p.h.+, 6-cyl., 3½-litre o.h.v. engine with twin carbs., 4-speed preselector gearbox with steering column control. Fluid transmission. Coil spring i.f.s. Tubeless tyres. Fitted heater. 4-door 5/6-seater. (Lady's Model with special equipment.)

- FOUR AND A HALF LITRE:* 100 m.p.h.+, 6-cyl., 4½-litre o.h.v. engine with twin carbs. 4-speed preselector gearbox with steering column control. Fluid transmission. Overdrive. Coil spring i.f.s. Fitted heater, 4-door 5/6-seater saloon.

- DK 400:* 90 m.p.h.+, 6-cyl., 4½-litre o.h.v. engine. 4-speed preselector gearbox with steering column control. Fluid transmission. Coil spring i.f.s., 8-seater luxury limousine.

EXCEPT for the Conquest and Conquest Century saloons, all the 1956 Daimler models are new. They are the 3½-litre One-o-Four, the 4½-litre saloon, the Conquest Drophead Coupé and the DK 400 Limousine. The One-o-Four replaces the

Daimler 4½-litre 4-light Saloon

Regency models and is a 100 m.p.h. car with a 137 b.h.p. 6-cylinder engine. Twin carburettors are fitted and the engine has an aluminium head. The usual Daimler 4-speed preselector gearbox and fluid flywheel afford great flexibility. The car has automatic chassis lubrication and standard features include heater and de-mister, new type semaphore trafficators and tubeless tyres. The One-o-Four Lady's model has a number of additional features such as a vanity case, a motoring rug, suitcases, a picnic case, a telescopic umbrella, an ice box, a shooting stick and power-operated windows.

The 100 m.p.h. 4½-litre saloon is built on the One-o-Four chassis and replaces the Sportsman models. It has an overdrive ratio for top gear, servo-assisted hydraulic brakes and a special low axle ratio. It is distinguishable on the road by its "wrap around" rear window and rear wheel spats. A feature of the luxurious interior fittings are the walnut burr occasional tables.

Daimler 2½-litre Drophead Coupé

Daimler 2½-litre "Conquest Century" Saloon

The 2½-litre Conquest and the 100 b.h.p. version of the same model—the Century—are continued without change. This is a six light saloon. The Century is identical in appearance to the Conquest, but has a twin carburettor engine. New this year is the Conquest Drophead Coupé, based on the 1955 Drophead Coupé and Roadster models. It is a 2/3-seater with a hood of washable greaseproof material, and a fitted heater. It is a low built car with square cut rear wings and two small humped scoops on the bonnet just behind the ridged Daimler radiator. The Drophead Coupé has the Century engine.

The new DK 400 Limousine is the largest standard production limousine in the British motor industry. It is an 8-seater and is powered by the 4½-litre 6-cylinder engine.

Daimler 3½-litre "One-o-Four"

Specifications

Model	c.c.	No. of Cyls.	Max. B.H.P.	Wheel Base	Max. Track	Length	Width	Turning Circle
CONQUEST ...	2,433	6	75	8′ 8″	4′ 4″	14′ 9½″	5′ 6″	33′
CENTURY ...	2,433	6	100	8′ 8″	4′ 4″	14′ 9½″	5′ 6″	33′
ONE-O-FOUR...	3,468	6	137	9′ 6″	4′ 9″	16′ 4″	5′ 10½″	42′
4½ LITRE ...	4,617	6	127	9′ 6″	4′ 9″	16′ 4″	5′ 10¾″	42′
DK.400 LIMOUSINE...	4,617	6	127	10′ 10″	5′ 3″	18′ 1″	6′ 4½″	45′

Total U.K. Prices

CONQUEST SALOON ..	£1,600 7s. 0d.
CENTURY SALOON ..	£1,759 7s. 0d.
DROPHEAD COUPÉ ..	£2,041 7s. 0d.
ONE-O-FOUR SALOON	£2,828 17s. 0d.
ONE-O-FOUR LADY'S MODEL	£3,158 17s. 2d.
4½-LITRE SALOON ..	£3,441 5s. 0d.
DK 400 LIMOUSINE	£4,190 17s. 0d.

Daimler DK.400 Limousine

Ford

Ford Motor Co., Ltd., Dagenham.

- POPULAR: 60 m.p.h.+, 4-cyl., 1·2-litre s.v. engine. 3-speed synchromesh gearbox with central control. Transverse leaf springs front and rear. 2-door, 4-light, 4-seater saloon.
- ANGLIA: 65 m.p.h.+, 4-cyl., 1·2-litre s.v. engine. 3-speed synchromesh gearbox with central control. Coil spring i.f.s. 2-door, 4-light, 4-seater saloon or de-luxe saloon.*
- PREFECT: 65 m.p.h.+, 4-cyl., 1·2-litre s.v. engine. 3-speed synchromesh gearbox with central control. Coil spring i.f.s. 4-door, 4-light, 4-seater saloon or de-luxe saloon.*
- *ESCORT: Details as for Anglia, but 2-door, 6-light, 4-seater estate car.
- *SQUIRE: Details as for Prefect, but 2-door, 6-light, 4-seater estate car.
- CONSUL: 70 m.p.h.+, 4-cyl., 1½-litre o.h.v. engine, 3-speed synchromesh gearbox. Steering column control. Coil spring i.f.s. 4-door, 4-light, 5/6-seater saloon or convertible.
- ZEPHYR: 80 m.p.h.+, 6-cyl., 2¼-litre o.h.v. engine, 3-speed synchromesh gearbox. Optional overdrive. Steering column control. Coil spring i.f.s. 4-door, 4-light, 5/6-seater saloon or convertible.
- ZODIAC: Luxury version of Zephyr with increased output.

THE Ford range for 1956 includes four new models—a de-luxe version of the Anglia and Prefect and two estate cars, the Escort and the Squire. Otherwise the 1955 models are continued without change. The Popular is claimed by its makers to be the cheapest car in the world at a basic price of £275. It is a combination of the Anglia body and the Prefect 10 h.p. engine of previous years. It has a top speed of over 60 m.p.h. and petrol consumption of up to 40 m.p.g. The equipment is necessarily a little austere at the price; there is a single windscreen wiper, twin tail and stop lights combined with reflectors and an interior jacking system. Transverse leaf springs are used at front and rear.

The Anglia and Prefect models are both powered by a similar engine to that used in the Popular, but with a higher output. The usual Ford three-speed gearbox is fitted in conjunction with a hydraulically operated clutch. Both cars have a top speed of more than 65 m.p.h., and petrol consumption at cruising speeds of about 45 m.p.g. They both have full width bodies. The Anglia, with a horizontal radiator grille, is the two-door model. The four-door Prefect has an oblong vertical grille rather like that of the Consul. Both cars have independent front suspension. The de-luxe models, available for the first time this year, have a newly designed facia panel, two-tone upholstery in P.V.C. or leather and other additions. Externally they are distinguishable by a full length chromium strip and the de-luxe Anglia has a new chromium grille and bumpers.

Ford Zephyr Six

The new estate cars are the Escort and the Squire, based respectively on the de-luxe Anglia and the de-luxe Prefect. Large windows in the side panels give excellent all round visibility and both models have an opening tail gate and rear window.

The 4-cylinder Consul and the 6-cylinder Zephyr are continued without change. Both have full width bodies, and the Consul is recognizable by its oblong radiator grille with vertical slats. The

Ford Escort

Above : Ford
Anglia de-luxe

Left : Ford
Popular

Below : Ford
Prefect de-luxe

Above : Ford
Squire

Right : Interior
of Ford Prefect
de-luxe

Below : Ford
Consul

Zephyr's grille is of horizontal slats. The petrol consumption range of the Consul is 24-28 m.p.g. The more powerful Zephyr has a petrol consumption of 23 to 26 m.p.g. The Zodiac is a luxury version of the Zephyr with fitted heater, fog lamps and other equipment.

Specifications

Model	c.c.	No. of Cyls.	Max. B.H.P.	Wheel Base	Max. Track	Length	Width	Turning Circle
POPULAR ...	1,172	4	30.1	7' 6"	3' 9"	12' 8¼"	4' 8½"	34' 9"
ANGLIA ...	1,172	4	36	7' 3"	4'	12' 7¼"	5' 0⅜"	33' 6"
PREFECT ...	1,172	4	36	7' 3"	4'	12' 7¼"	5' 0⅜"	33' 6"
ESCORT ...	1,172	4	36	7' 3"	4'	11' 9"	5'	32' 9"
SQUIRE ...	1,172	4	36	7' 3"	4'	11' 10"	5'	32' 9"
CONSUL ...	1,508	4	47	8' 4"	4' 2"	13' 8¼"	5' 4"	40' 6"
ZEPHYR ...	2,262	6	68	8' 8"	4' 2"	14' 4"	5' 4"	41' 6"
ZODIAC ...	2,262	6	71	8' 8"	4' 2"	14' 4"	5' 4"	41' 6"

Total U.K. Prices

POPULAR	£413 17s. 0d.
ANGLIA	£541 7s. 0d.
ESCORT ESTATE CAR	£622 7s. 0d.
PREFECT	£593 17s. 0d.
SQUIRE ESTATE CAR	£668 16s. 0d.
CONSUL	£706 7s. 0d.
CONSUL CONVERTIBLE	£856 7s. 0d.
ZEPHYR SIX SALOON	£799 7s. 0d.
ZEPHYR CONVERTIBLE	£1,016 17s. 0d.
ZODIAC	£901 7s. 0d.

Frazer Nash

**A.F.N. Ltd.,
Falcon Works,
London Road,
Isleworth.**

● 130 m.p.h., or 110 m.p.h. versions of the 2-litre, 6-cyl., o.h.v. engine. 3 carbs., 4-speed synchromesh gearbox. Central lever. Sebring 2-seater Gran Sport. Le Mans Fixed Head Coupé and Targa Florio Turismo models.

THE Frazer Nash is a hand-built sports car with a considerable reputation in sporting events going back for many years. The current models include the Sebring Gran Sport open two-seater with all enveloping bodywork, the Le Mans Fixed Head

Frazer Nash Sebring

Coupé, and the Targa Florio Gran Turismo. The Sebring, designed for serious competition work, has the 2-litre, 6-cylinder engine which gives a top speed of between 130 and 140 m.p.h. It is available at extra cost with a De Dion rear axle. The Coupé, with the same engine and performance, has unusually generous luggage accommodation for a car of this type. The Targa Florio is built to a more standard pattern and the 2-litre engine gives a top speed of about 110 m.p.h. A new Frazer Nash is to be introduced in the near future powered by a V.8 engine—probably in two forms, 2·6-litres and 3-litres. Frazer Nash cars have achieved notable successes at Le Mans, and are the only British make ever to have won the gruelling Targa Florio road race.

Specifications

Model	c.c.	No. of Cyls.	Max. B.H.P.	Wheel Base	Max. Track	Length	Width	Turning Circle
SEBRING ...	1,971	6	140	8'	4' 4"	13' 5"	5' 2"	32'
LE MANS FIXED HEAD ...	1,971	6	140	8'	4' 4"	13'	4' 10"	28'
TARGA FLORIO TURISMO ...	1,971	6	105	8'	4' 4"	13'	5' 3½"	28'

Total U.K. Prices

SEBRING	..	..	..	..	..	£3,376 7s. 0d.
LE MANS FIXED HEAD	..	..	..	..	£3,751 7s. 0d.
TARGA FLORIO	..	..	..	..	£2,475 12s. 0d.

Hillman

Hillman Motor Co., Ltd.,

(Rootes Group),

Ryton-on-Dunsmore,

Coventry.

- MINX: 75 m.p.h., 4-cyl., 1·4 litre o.h.v. engine, 4-speed, synchromesh gearbox. Steering column change. Coil spring i.f.s. 4-door, 4-light saloon; 2-door hardtop (Californian) and 2-door convertible models.

- HUSKY: 65 m.p.h., 4-cyl., 1·3-litre s.v. engine. 4-speed synchromesh gearbox. Central change. Coil spring i.f.s. 2-door, 4-seater, short wheelbase utility. (Also Hillman Estate Car on Minx chassis.)

THE principal changes in the Hillman programme for 1956 are the introduction of two colour finishes and the fitting of the 1,390 c.c. overhead valve engine—already used in the Minx de-luxe—to the Minx Special saloon, and the Estate Car in place of the 1,265 c.c. side-valve unit. The tough, dual purpose, utility Husky—introduced last year—is thus the only Hillman to continue with the side valve engine.

The overhead valve engine has a top speed of about 75 m.p.h. and lively acceleration. The side valve unit gives a maximum speed of more than 65 m.p.h., but is more economical and the Husky can claim petrol consumption of 40 m.p.g. at cruising

Hillman Husky

36

Hillman Minx

speeds. The de-luxe and Special Minx saloons have a 4-door, 4-light body. The Californian is an attractive hardtop with "wraparound" rear window. All Hillmans may be recognized by the distinctive oval radiator grille with its horizontal bar. The Minx de-luxe this year has a revised boot lid with a horizontal tapered fairing which incorporates the rear number plate lamp.

Hillmans have a 4-speed synchromesh gearbox with a change lever mounted on the steering column—the Husky alone has a central lever. Front suspension on all models is by independent coil springs, and semi-elliptic springs are used at the rear.

Hillman Californian

Specifications

Model	c.c.	No. of Cyls.	Max. B.H.P.	Wheel Base	Max. Track	Length	Width	Turning Circle
MINX DE LUXE CALIFORNIAN SPECIAL SALOON ...	1,390	4	47	7′ 9″	4′ 0⅜″	13′ 3½″	5′ 3½″	33′
ESTATE CAR ...	1,390	4	47	7′ 9″	4′ 0⅜″	13′ 8″	5′ 3½″	33′
HUSKY ...	1,265	4	35	7′	4′ 0⅜″	12′ 2″	5′ 2″	31′

Total U.K. Prices

SPECIAL SALOON	..	..	..	..	..	£706	7s. 0d.
DE-LUXE SALOON	..	..	..	..	..	£743	17s. 0d.
CONVERTIBLE COUPÉ	..	..	..	..		£811	7s. 0d.
CALIFORNIAN HARDTOP	..	..	..	..		£826	7s. 0d.
ESTATE CAR..	..	..	..	..		£848	17s. 0d.
HUSKY	..	..	..	..	..	£623	17s. 0d.

Humber

Humber Ltd.,

(Rootes Group),

Ryton-on-Dunsmore,

Coventry.

- HAWK: 80 m.p.h., 4-cyl., 2¼-litre o.h.v. engine. 4-speed synchromesh gearbox with optional overdrive. Steering column change. Coil spring i.f.s., 4/5-seater, 4-door saloon or touring limousine. Estate Car.*

- SUPER SNIPE: 90 m.p.h., 6-cyl., 4·1-litre o.h.v. engine. 4-speed synchromesh gearbox with optional overdrive. Steering column change. Coil spring i.f.s. 6-seater, 4-door saloon or touring limousine.

THE new addition to the Humber range for 1956 is the Hawk Estate Car, the earliest version of which was delivered to Sir Winston Churchill before the Motor Show. This has a 4-door body on a strengthened version of the Hawk chassis, and it can carry five passengers and 2¾ cwt. of luggage. The rear door is hinged at the bottom like a tailboard—an unusual arrangement for an estate car.

The Humber Hawk family saloon has an overhead valve, 4-cylinder engine. Overdrive in top gear is an optional feature.

Humber Super Snipe

This combination gives a top speed of over 80 m.p.h. and sharp acceleration. The distinctive Humber radiator is narrow and rounded with a vertical grille and a low brow. There are separate intakes on either side of the radiator and these incorporate the side lamps. Flashing direction indicators are fitted. A touring limousine is also available.

The Super Snipe is powered by the Blue Riband 6-cylinder overhead valve engine. Overdrive is available on the Super Snipe this year, and the top speed is over 90 m.p.h. The model is available as either a six-seater four-door saloon, or as a touring limousine with a glass partition behind the front seats. The coil spring independent front suspension incorporates some improvements this

Humber Hawk Saloon

Two views of the Humber Hawk Estate Car

year, and a new Zenith-Stromberg carburettor is fitted with a manually controlled choke instead of the former thermostatically controlled choke. A redesigned rear number plate mounting is the principal external change, but all Humber Hawks and Super Snipes are now available with two colour paintwork.

Specifications

Model	c.c.	No. of Cyls.	Max. B.H.P.	Wheel Base	Max. Track	Length	Width	Turning Circle
HAWK & HAWK ESTATE CAR	2,267	4	75	8′ 9½″	4′ 9″	15′ 1½″	6′	37′
SUPER SNIPE ...	4,139	6	122	9′ 7¾″	4′ 9″	16′ 5″	6′ 1½″	43′

Total U.K. Prices

HAWK SALOON	£1,073 17s. 0d.
HAWK TOURING LIMOUSINE	£1,193 17s. 0d.
HAWK ESTATE CAR	£1,328 7s. 0d.
SUPER SNIPE SALOON	£1,643 17s. 0d.
SUPER SNIPE LIMOUSINE	£1,763 17s. 0d·

Jaguar

Jaguar Cars Ltd.,

Coventry.

- 2·4 LITRE:* 100 m.p.h.+, 6-cyl., 2·4 litre twin o.h.c. engine. Twin carbs. 4-speed synchromesh gearbox. Central control. Overdrive optional. Fitted heater and fog lamps on special equipment model. Coil and wishbone i.f.s. Cantilever half-elliptic rear springs. 4-door, 5-seater saloon.

- X.K.140: 140 m.p.h., 6-cyl., 3½-litre twin o.h.c. engine. Twin carbs. 4-speed synchromesh gearbox. Central control. Overdrive optional. Torsion bar i.f.s. 2-door, 2-seater Sports.

- MARK VII: 100 m.p.h.+, 6-cyl., 3½-litre engine similar to XK 140. 4-speed synchromesh gearbox. Central control. Overdrive and automatic transmission optional extras. 4-door 5-seater saloon.

A NEW Jaguar saloon—the 2·4-litre—has been added to the Jaguar range for 1956. The newcomer, like its famous stable companions the Mark VII and the XK.140 Sports, is a 100 m.p.h. model and is available in two versions of which the special

Jaguar Mark VII

equipment model has such fittings as heater, fog lamps, tachometer, screen washers and a folding centre arm-rest. The 2·4-litre is of integral construction and has a radiator similar in appearance to the XK.140. It is a full five-seater saloon with spats over the rear wheels. Front suspension is by coil spring and wishbones. At the rear, cantilever leaf springs are used. The engine is a scaled down version of the famous XK.140 and has twin Solex carburettors.

The XK.140 Sports is continued this year with the Mark VII powered by the same 6-cylinder, 3½-litre engine which gives the sports model a top speed of up to 140 m.p.h. Three versions of the Sports are offered—the 2-seater, the coupé, and the convertible (illustrated). The narrow pear-shaped radiator grille is surmounted by the " roaring jaguar " badge. The rear wheels are partly covered. The fine Mark VII, 5-seater saloon has a long bonnet and a slightly pointed radiator with a vertical grille and a winged

Jaguar 2·4 litre

Jaguar XK 140 Drophead Coupé

badge. Dunlop tubeless tyres are a standard fitting, and automatic transmission is an optional extra, as is overdrive.

The famous D Type Jaguar, victor at Le Mans in 1955, is also offered to the public as a competition model.

Specifications

Model	c.c.	No. of Cyls.	Max. B.H.P.	Wheel Base	Max. Track	Length	Width	Turning Circle
2.4 LITRE ...	2,483	6	112	8' 11⅜"	4' 6⅝"	15' 0¾"	5' 6¾"	33' 6"
XK140	3,442	6	190	8' 6"	4' 3½"	14' 8"	5' 4½"	33'
MARK VII ...	3,442	6	190	10'	4' 10"	16' 4½"	6' 1"	36'
D TYPE ...	3,442	6	250	7' 6"	4' 2"	12' 10"	5' 5"	32'

Total U.K. Prices

2·4 LITRE	£1,343 17s. 0d.
XK.140 SPORTS	£1,692 12s. 0d.
XK.140 FIXED HEAD	£1,711 7s. 0d.
XK.140 DROPHEAD	£1,741 7s. 0d.
MARK VII	£1,711 7s. 0d.
D TYPE	£3,878 17s. 0d.

Jensen

**Jensen Motors Ltd.,
West Bromwich,
Staffs.**

- INTERCEPTOR:—100 m.p.h.+, 6-cyl., o.h.v., 4-litre engine. 4-speed synchromesh gearbox. Central control. Overdrive (optional). Heater-demister.

- 541, 2-door, 4-seater plastic saloon. Interceptor, 2-door, 4/5-seater saloon or 2-door convertible.

THE plastic bodied Jensen 541 saloon has a maximum speed of 115 m.p.h. and over. The low compact sports saloon body has a curved tail with a wide rear screen and a spacious rear locker. There is an oval radiator duct with an adjustable centre flap, and wire wheels are fitted. The car has a dry weight of 24 cwts., and is powered by a basically Austin 6-cylinder overhead valve 4-litre engine, served by three carburettors. Laycock-de-Normanville

Jensen Interceptor

overdrive is an optional feature, and when it is fitted a fuel consumption of about 24 m.p.g. at fast cruising speeds is claimed. The makers also claim acceleration from 0 to 30 m.p.h. in 4·1 seconds, 50 m.p.h. in 8·4 seconds, 90 m.p.h. in 24·5 seconds.

The Interceptor saloon, the de-luxe saloon, and the convertible models, are continued this year and these also have a top speed with overdrive of over 100 m.p.h. The engine is again the Austin 4-litre, 6-cylinder, but on the Interceptor a single carburettor is used. The car is provided with an adjustable steering column. Independent front suspension is by coil springs and wishbones, and there are long semi-elliptic leaf springs at the rear. Girling hydraulic brakes are fitted. The principal change in the external appearance of the Interceptor in 1956, are the ventilators at the

Jensen 541

sides of the front wings to allow warm under bonnet airs to escape. Front apertures are provided, as last year, for brake cooling. The body is made of aluminium alloy.

Specifications

Model	c.c.	No. of Cyls.	Max. B.H.P.	Wheel Base	Max. Track	Length	Width	Turning Circle
541	3,993	6	130	8′ 9″	4′ 3⅜″	14′ 8″	5′ 3″	34′
INTERCEPTOR	3,993	6	130	9′ 4½″	4′ 9⅜″	15′ 10″	5′ 6″	38′

Total U.K. Prices

541	..	..	..	..	..	£1,928 17s.	0d.
541 SPECIAL	..	..	..	..	..	£2,272 12s.	0d.
INTERCEPTOR	..	..	..	..	..	£2,651 7s.	0d.
INTERCEPTOR DE-LUXE AND DROPHEAD				..		£2,701 7s.	0d.

Lagonda

Lagonda Ltd.,

Feltham,

Middlesex.

● 100 m.p.h.+, 6-cyl., 3-litre twin o.h.c. engine. Twin S.U. carbs. Fitted radio, heater and demister. Servo-assisted brakes. 4-speed synchromesh gearbox, 4-wheel independent suspension. 4-seater, 4-door saloon or 2-door drophead coupé.

ANOTHER product of the David Brown organization, the Lagonda is powered by the same engine as the Aston Martin D.B.2-4—a 6-cylinder, 3-litre, of overhead camshaft design which gives a top speed of over 100 m.p.h. The petrol consumption range is 20 to 23 m.p.g. The Lagonda has a finely engineered

45

3-litre 4-door Lagonda

cruciform chassis and all four wheels are independently sprung. For recognition features note the long bonnet and curved nose with its pear-shaped radiator grille. Built-in hydraulic jacks are fitted, and standard fittings include a radio, heating and demisting unit, twin fog lamps, two-speed windscreen wipers and windscreen washers. A 4-door saloon and a drophead coupé—both with Tickford coachwork—are available.

Lagonda 2-door Drophead Coupé

Specifications

Model	c.c.	No. of Cyls.	Max. B.H.P.	Wheel Base	Max. Track	Length	Width	Turning Circle
4-DOOR SALOON ...	2,922	6	140	9' 5½"	4' 8¾"	16' 4"	5' 9½"	38'

Total U.K. Prices

LAGONDA FOUR-DOOR SALOON ..   ..   ..   £3,901   7s.   0d.

LAGONDA DROPHEAD COUPÉ   ..   ..   ..   £4,051   7s.   0d.

Lanchester

**Lanchester Motor Co.,
Ltd.,**

Coventry.

● SPRITE: 80 m.p.h.+, 4-cyl., 1½-litre, o.h.v. engine. 4-speed, fully automatic gearbox by throttle control with over-riding lever on steering column. Mechanical drive in all gears. Torsion bar i.f.s. 4/5-seater, 4-door saloon.

A NEW version of the Sprite, the prototype of which appeared at the 1954 Motor Show, is now coming into production. This is the first medium size car to be offered with an automatic gearbox. The box used on the Sprite is the British Hobbs.

Lanchester Sprite Saloon

47

Fully automatic control is achieved by the throttle only, and the Sprite, therefore, has only two pedals—throttle and brake. There is a selector lever on the steering wheel to over-ride the gearbox if necessary. The 4-cylinder overhead valve engine gives a top speed of over 80 m.p.h. with a petrol consumption of 30 m.p.g. Coil spring front suspension used on the prototype is now replaced by torsion bars and an anti-roll bar is also fitted. The body is similar in appearance to that of the 2½-litre Daimlers, and the Sprite is a comfortable 4/5-seater.

Specifications

Model	c.c.	No. of Cyls.	Max. B.H.P.	Wheel Base	Max. Track	Length	Width	Turning Circle
SPRITE	1,622	4	60	8′ 4″	4′ 4″	14′ 4″	5′ 6¾″	33′

Total U.K. Prices

SPRITE   ..   ..   £1,300   7s.   0d.

M.G.

M.G. Car Co., Ltd.,

Abingdon-on-Thames,

Berkshire.

- SERIES A:* 90 m.p.h., 4-cyl., 1½-litre, push-rod o.h.v. engine. Twin S.U. carbs. 4-speed gearbox. Central control. I.f.s. by coil spring. Rigid rear axle. 2-door, 2-seater tourer.

- MAGNETTE: 80 m.p.h., 4-cyl., 1½-litre push-rod o.h.v. engine. Twin carbs. 4-speed gearbox. Central control; i.f.s. by coil springs. Rigid rear axle. 4-door, 4-seater saloon.

TO replace the long–famous T series of M.G. Midgets, a completely new two-seater sports car has been introduced by the Nuffield Organization for 1956. It is based on the prototype M.G. Ex 182, which ran at Le Mans and in the Tourist Trophy Race. The 1½-litre, 4-cylinder engine is developed from the B.M.C. B. Series engine already used in the M.G. Magnette, the Austin A.50 and the Morris Oxford. It is served by twin S.U. carburettors with separate air cleaners. For the first time a full width body is employed, and the seats are low down between the chassis members and the propeller shaft. The small oblong radiator grille retains the M.G. centre bar and octagonal name plate. The redesigned body has permitted the inclusion of a luggage boot.

M.G.A. Sports

Left-hand or right-hand drive is obtainable, and extra equipment includes radio, heater, fog lamps, tonneau cover and a telescopic steering wheel.

M.G. Magnette

The Magnette full four-seater saloon is continued for 1956 without change. The 4-cylinder, 1½-litre engine has twin carburettors. Independent front suspension is by coil springs, with telescopic dampers. The 4-door, 4-light body has rear quarter lights, and drilled disc wheels are fitted. This model was first introduced in 1954.

Specifications

Model	c.c.	No. of Cyls.	Max. B.H.P.	Wheel Base	Max. Track	Length	Width	Turning Circle
SERIES A ...	1,489	4	68	7' 10"	4' 0¾"	13'	4' 10"	28'
MAGNETTE ...	1,489	4	60	8' 6"	4' 3"	14' 1"	5' 3"	32'

Total U.K. Prices

SERIES A	..	..	..	..	..	£893 17s. 0d.
MAGNETTE	..	..	..	..	..	£968 17s. 0d.

Morgan

Morgan Motor Co.,

Malvern Link,

Worcestershire.

- PLUS FOUR: 100 m.p.h., 4-cyl., 2-litre o.h.v. T.R.2 engine with twin S.U. carbs., or 85 m.p.h. 4-cyl., 2-litre o.h.v. Vanguard engine. 4-speed synchromesh gearbox. Central control. Coil spring i.f.s.; 2- or 4-seater tourers, or 2- or 4-seater coupés.

- 4/4 SERIES II:* 70 m.p.h., 4-cyl., 1·2-litre s.v. Ford engine. 3-speed synchromesh gearbox. Central control. Coil spring i.f.s. 2-door Sports.

A FIRM with a tradition of sports car construction dating back to 1912, the Morgan Motor Co., of Malvern Link, Worcestershire, offer a new and cheaper sports car this year in addition to their well-established Plus Four models. The new car, the 4/4 Series II, is powered by a Ford 10 h.p. engine which provides a top speed of 77 m.p.h. Although a little lower, the body closely resembles the body of the Plus Four 2-seater model. The Plus Four Series consists of 2-and 4-seater tourers and coupés, with the

Morgan 2-seater Tourer

option of the 2-litre Vanguard engine or the more potent T.R.2
engine which provides a top speed of over 100 m.p.h. and very
rapid acceleration. Note the distinctive curved Morgan radiator
with its vertical grille, and the drilled wheels.

Specifications

Model	c.c.	No. of Cyls.	Max. B.H.P.	Wheel Base	Max. Track	Length	Width	Turning Circle
PLUS FOUR ...	2,088	4	68	8′	3′ 11″	12′	4′ 7½″	34′
PLUS FOUR T.R.2	1,991	4	90	8′	3′ 11″	12′	4′ 7½″	34′
4/4 SERIES II ...	1,172	4	36	8′	3′ 11″	12′	4′ 8″	33′

Total U.K. Prices

T.R.2 TWO-SEATER TOURER	£893 17s. 0d.
T.R.2 FOUR-SEATER TOURER	£916 7s. 0d.
VANGUARD FOUR-SEATER TOURER	£875 7s. 0d.
T.R.2 TWO-SEATER COUPÉ	£961 7s. 0d.
VANGUARD TWO-SEATER COUPÉ	£916 7s. 0d.
T.R.2 4/4 SERIES II TWO-SEATER	£677 7s. 0d.

Morris

Morris Motors Ltd.,

Nuffield Organisation,

Cowley,

Oxford.

- MINOR: 70 m.p.h., $\frac{3}{4}$-litre, 4-cyl., o.h.v. engine. 4-speed synchromesh gearbox with central change. Torsion bar i.f.s. 2- or 4-door, 4-seater saloons. 2-door, 4-seater convertible or Travellers Car in standard or deluxe form.

- OXFORD: 80 m.p.h., $1\frac{1}{2}$-litre, 4-cyl., o.h.v. engine. 4-speed synchromesh gearbox with steering column change. Torsion bar i.f.s. 4-door, 6-seater saloon.

- COWLEY: 70 m.p.h., 1·2-litre o.h.v. engine. 4-speed synchromesh gearbox with steering column change. Torsion bar i.f.s. 4-door, 6-seater saloon.

- ISIS:* 85 m.p.h., $2\frac{1}{2}$-litre, 6-cyl., o.h.v. engine. 4-speed synchromesh gearbox with steering column change. Torsion bar i.f.s. 4-door, 6-seater saloon.

THE Morris range for 1956 consists of four family models, the Minor, the Cowley, the Oxford and the Isis. The Minor (Series II) is continued without major change for yet another year, and it remains one of the most popular small cars in the world. The 4-cylinder o.h.v. engine is similar to that used in the Austin Seven, and gives a top speed of between 65 and 70 m.p.h. The torsion bar front suspension, used on all Morris models, affords excellent road-holding ability. Petrol consumption is more than 40 m.p.g. The monoconstruction body is available either in

Morris Isis Saloon

Morris Oxford Series II

saloon or touring form and there is a choice of 2-door or 4-door models. There is also an estate car—the Travellers Car.

The Oxford (Series II) is a 4-door, 6-seater saloon with a lively performance and a petrol consumption of about 30 m.p.g. Note the double-tier radiator grille, the full width body, and the humped air scoop for the heater unit. There is also a Travellers Car version. The Cowley is a cheaper version of the Oxford with a slightly smaller 4-cylinder engine which provides a lively performance combined with economy.

The Isis is the new 6-cylinder Morris. Similar to the Oxford and the Cowley in appearance, it is a full 6-seater, and the powerful $2\frac{1}{2}$-litre engine gives a high top speed. The Travellers' Car version of the Isis will seat six adults and two children.

Morris Minor Saloon

Specifications

Model	c.c.	No. of Cyls.	Max. B.H.P.	Wheel Base	Max. Track	Length	Width	Turning Circle
MINOR	800	4	30	7' 2"	4' 2⅜"	12' 4"	5' 1"	33' 1½"
OXFORD ...	1,489	4	52	8' 11"	4' 5½"	14' 3"	5' 5"	35' 6"
COWLEY ...	1,200	4	42	8' 1"	4' 5½"	14' 1"	5' 5"	35' 6"
ISIS	2,639	6	86	8' 11½"	4' 5½"	14 10"	5' 5"	

Total U.K. Prices

MINOR TWO-DOOR SALOON	£560 17s. 0d.
MINOR CONVERTIBLE	£560 17s. 0d.
MINOR FOUR-DOOR SALOON	£593 17s. 0d.
MINOR TRAVELLER	£635 2s. 0d.
MINOR TRAVELLER DE-LUXE	£659 2s. 0d.
OXFORD SALOON	£788 17s. 0d.
OXFORD TRAVELLER	£871 7s. 0d.
COWLEY SALOON	£743 17s. 0d.
ISIS SALOON..	£848 17s. 0d.
ISIS SALOON DE-LUXE	£893 17s. 0d.
ISIS TRAVELLER	£1,013 17s. 0d.

Morris Minor Traveller

Riley

**Riley Motors Ltd.,
Nuffield Organisation,
Abingdon-on-Thames,
Berkshire.**

● PATHFINDER: 100 m.p.h.+, 2½-litre, 6-cyl., o.h.v. engine. Twin S.U. carbs. 4-speed synchromesh gearbox with right-hand change lever. Vacuum servo-assisted brakes, torsion bar i.f.s., coil springs at rear, 4-door, 4/5-seater saloon.

THE 2½-litre Pathfinder saloon is the only Riley model in production this year. The 6-cylinder high performance engine has inclined overhead valves and a hemispherical head and provides this luxury saloon with a top speed of more than 100 m.p.h. Independent suspension is provided by torsion bar at the front and coil springs at the rear. Either bucket or bench type

Riley Pathfinder

front seats can be fitted. The Pathfinder is a 4-door, 4-light saloon, with the typical Riley radiator grille, built-in headlamps, a jutting boot, and a curved one-piece windscreen and rear screen.

Specifications

Model	c.c.	No. of Cyls.	Max. B.H.P.	Wheel Base	Max. Track	Length	Width	Turning Circle
PATHFINDER	2,443	6	102	9′ 5½″	4′ 6″	15′ 3″	5′ 7″	36′

Total U.K. Prices

PATHFINDER SALOON .. .. £1,313 17s. 0d.

Rolls-Royce

**Rolls-Royce Ltd.,
(Motor Car Division),
14-15, Conduit Street,
London, W.1.**

- SILVER CLOUD:* 100 m.p.h., 6-cyl.,
  4·9-litre engine. Twin S.U. carbs.
  Automatic gearbox. Servo-assisted
  brakes. Fitted heater and ventilator
  system. 5/6-seater, 4-door saloon.
- SILVER WRAITH: 100 m.p.h., 6-cyl.,
  4·9-litre engine. Automatic gearbox.
  Servo-assisted brakes. Fitted heater
  and ventilator system. Various coach
  built saloon and limousine bodies.

THE completely new Rolls–Royce—the Silver Cloud—lives up to the firm's reputation of dignity and excellence. The chassis frame is of welded steel construction, and a more powerful 6-cylinder engine provides silent and swift motive power. The engine follows long established Rolls–Royce design, having overhead inlet valves and side exhaust valves. The brake horsepower

Rolls Royce Silver Wraith

is not revealed. The engine is served by two S.U. carburettors of a new diaphragm type and the engine has an aluminium alloy cylinder head. The 4-speed automatic gearbox is a standard feature. Independent front suspension is by coil springs with hydraulic shock dampers and anti-roll rod. Semi-elliptic springs are used at the rear with electrically controlled dampers. The Silver Cloud has a 5/6-seater, 4-door saloon body which, in spite of its modern design, retains the traditional Rolls–Royce characteristics. The familiar radiator with its flat top and sloping shoulders, has the goddess mascot. The Silver Wraith is continued with the new and more powerful Rolls-Royce engine. A single Zenith carburettor is used on this model, and the independent front suspension is by helical springs with hydraulic shock dampers

Interior of Silver Cloud

and anti-roll bar. A number of saloon and limousine bodies by famous coachbuilding firms like Hooper, Park Ward and Mulliner are available.

Specifications

Model	c.c.	No. of Cyls.	Max. B.H.P.	Wheel Base	Max. Track	Length	Width	Turning Circle
SILVER CLOUD	4,887	6	—	10' 3"	5'	17' 8"	6' 2¾"	41' 8"
SILVER WRAITH (CHASSIS)	4,887	6	—	11'	5'	18' 2"	6' 5"	45' 6"

Rolls Royce Silver Cloud

SILVER CLOUD SALOON	£5.078 17s. 0d.
SILVER WRAITH HOOPER ENCLOSED LIMOUSINE	£7,943 17s. 0d.
PARK WARD TOURING SALOON	£7,756 7s. 0d.
MULLINER TOURING LIMOUSINE	£7,898 17s. 0d.

Rover

Rover Co., Ltd.,

Solihull,

Birmingham.

- "60": 4-cyl., 2-litre engine. Overhead inlet and side exhaust valves. 4-speed synchromesh gearbox with central control. Freewheel. 4/5-seater, 4-door, 4-light saloon.
- "75": 6-cyl., 2¼-litre engine of similar design.
- "90": 6-cyl., 2½-litre engine of similar design. Optional overdrive. Vacuum-assisted two-trailing shoe brakes.

THERE are only changes of detail in the Rover range of three cars for 1956. The "60" the "75" and the "90," are all similar in appearance and, in fact, the only difference is under the bonnet. The number by which each model is known represents the output of the engine. The "60" is powered by a 4-cylinder,

Rover "90" Saloon

2-litre engine, the " 75 " by a 6-cylinder, 2¼-litre engine, and the
" 90 " by a 6-cylinder, 2½-litre engine.

All three models have a " wraparound " rear window and a
jutting boot. The Rover may be recognized by its square radiator
grille bearing at the top the badge of a Norseman's sailing boat
set in a triangle. All three models have coil spring independent
front suspension, freewheel, a central gearchange and flashing
traffic indicators.

This year the " 90 " is offered with Laycock-de Normanville
overdrive as an optional feature. In this form the car has a top
speed of over 90 m.p.h., and a petrol consumption of 34 m.p.g. at
40 m.p.h. Another new feature in the biggest of the Rovers is two
trailing shoe brakes with vacuum assistance. On all models
separate front seats are available if preferred to the bench type.

Specifications

Model	c.c.	No. of Cyls.	Max. B.H.P.	Wheel Base	Max. Track	Length	Width	Turning Circle
" 60 "	1,997	4	60	9′ 3″	4′ 4″	14′ 10¼″	5′ 5⅝″	37′
" 75 "	2,230	6	80	9′ 3″	4′ 4″	14′ 10¼″	5′ 5⅝″	37′
" 90 "	2,638	6	93	9′ 3″	4′ 4″	14′ 10¼″	5′ 5⅝″	37′

Total U.K. Prices

" 60 " SALOON	..	..	..	..	..	£1,261	7s.	0d.
" 75 " SALOON	..	..	..	..	..	£1,373	17s.	0d.
" 90 " SALOON	..	..	..	..	..	£1,418	17s.	0d.
LAND ROVER	..	..	..	..	..	£968	17s.	0d.

Singer Hunter 75

Singer

Singer Motors Ltd.,

Coventry Road,

Birmingham.

- HUNTER: 75 m.p.h., 4-cyl., 1½-litre o.h.c. engine. 4-speed synchromesh gearbox with steering column or central control. Coil spring i.f.s. Fitted heater, screen washers, etc. 4-door, 4-seater, semi-plastic saloon.

- HUNTER S:* Similar specifications, but less fully equipped. Steering column or central control.

- HUNTER 75:* 90 m.p.h., 4-cyl., 1½-litre twin o.h.c. engine with twin carbs. 4-speed synchromesh gearbox. Steering column or central control. Coil spring i.f.s. Fitted heater, screen washers, etc. 4-door, 4/5-seater semi-plastic saloon.

- ROADSTER: 75 m.p.h., 4-cyl., 1½-litre o.h.c. engine. Twin carbs. optional. 4-speed synchromesh gearbox with central control. Coil spring i.f.s. 2-door, 2-seater sports.

THE Hunter saloon was introduced last year to replace the S.M.1500, and this year it is joined by two companions, the Hunter 75 and the Hunter S. The " 75" has a more powerful twin overhead camshaft engine and the S model is cheaper and less fully equipped. The cars are notable for their semi-plastic construction—the bonnet top and valances joining the bonnet to the wings are made of glass fibre impregnated with polyester resins. The Hunter and the Hunter S have the 1½-litre power unit similar to that formerly used in the S.M.1500. The new 75 b.h.p. engine is of 1,496 c.c. capacity, and is served by twin Solex carburettors. All three models have independent coil spring front suspension and semi-elliptic leaf springs at the rear. The Hunter S may be distinguished by its lack of chromium trim. The 75 and the Hunter also have fluted wing edges. The radiator has a vertical

Singer Roadster

grille. The Hunter and Hunter 75 models have heater, demister, screen washers, fog lamps and rim embellishers as standard equipment. Tubeless tyres are fitted on all models and on the S model the makers have taken advantage of this to leave the spare wheel out of the standard equipment.

The well-known Roadster Sports model is continued with the choice of single or twin carburettors.

Specifications

Model	c.c.	No. of Cyls.	Max. B.H.P.	Wheel Base	Max. Track	Length	Width	Turning Circle
HUNTER HUNTER S* ...	1,497	4	50	8' 11½"	4' 3"	14' 9"	5' 3"	33'
HUNTER 75 ...	1,496	4	75	8' 11½"	4' 3"	14' 9"	5' 3"	33'
ROADSTER ...	1,497	4	50	7' 7"	3' 10¾"	12' 9"	4' 10"	33'

* With two carbs the b.h.p. is 58

Total U.K. Prices

HUNTER S SALOON	..	..	..	..	£919 7s. 0d.
HUNTER SALOON	..	..	..	..	£1,033 4s. 0d.
HUNTER 75 SALOON	..	..	..	..	£1,217 17s. 0d.
ROADSTER	..	..	..	..	£766 7s. 0d.

Standard

Standard Motor Co., Ltd.,

Coventry.

- VANGUARD III:* 80 m.p.h., 4-cyl., 2-litre o.h.v. engine. 3-speed synchromesh gearbox with steering column change. Optional overdrive. Coil spring and wishbone i.f.s. 4-door, 4-light, 5/6-seater saloon. Fitted heater. Also 5/6-seater Estate Car.

- FAMILY EIGHT AND SUPER EIGHT: 60 m.p.h., 4-cyl., 800 c.c. o.h.v. engine. 4-speed synchromesh gearbox with central change. Coil spring and wishbone i.f.s. 4-door, 4-light, 4-seater saloon. (SUPER EIGHT includes heater, etc.).

- SUPER TEN: 68 m.p.h., 4-cyl., 950 c.c. o.h.v. engine. 4-speed gearbox with central change. Coil spring and wishbone i.f.s. 4-door, 4-light, 4-seater saloon fitted heater, (or 4-seater, 6-light, Good Companion estate car).

A NEW version of the famous Standard Vanguard family saloon—the Vanguard III—is the principal change in the Standard programme for 1956. The engine is the famous 2-litre, 4-cylinder unit, but the body has been redesigned. This

Standard Eight Saloon

has a jutting boot, a " wraparound " rear screen, heavy bumpers front and rear, and an American type radiator grille, with the side lights incorporated in the horizontal central bar. There is an air scoop for the heater unit just in front of the curved windscreen. The Vanguard is a 4-door, 5/6-seater, with a top speed of about 84 m.p.h. At high speed touring the fuel consumption is claimed to be 26-32 m.p.g. at 50 m.p.h. The Phase II, 2-litre Estate Car, is continued this year and the Phase II Saloon is available with the Diesel engine.

The Standard small car range this year consists of the Family Eight, the Super Eight, the Super Ten and the Ten Good Companion Estate Car. The Family Eight has already proved itself to be an economical and sturdy performer in the small car class. The overhead valve engine has a top speed of over 60 m.p.h., and fuel consumption is claimed to be 57 m.p.g. at 30 m.p.h. and 42 m.p.g. at 50 m.p.h. The car is not quite so utility as it was when first introduced, and it now has wind–up windows, press button door locks, trimmed doors and self-cancelling flashing direction indicators. Twin windscreen wipers, chromium-plated hub plates, and upholstered seats with Dunlop overlay are also fitted this year. The Super Eight has a fully trimmed interior, a fitted heater, and various other items which are extras on the Family Eight. The Super Ten has a top speed of about 68 m.p.h., and petrol consumption is 53 m.p.g. at 30 m.p.h., and 41 m.p.g. at 50 m.p.h. On the Ten the boot has an exterior opening lid and standard equipment

Standard Ten Saloon

includes a windscreen washer. The Ten Good Companion estate car has two goods doors at the rear and will carry 4 cwt. of goods with two passengers or 1 cwt. with four passengers.

Standard Ten Estate Car

Standard Vanguard III

Specifications

Model	c.c.	No. of Cyls.	Max. B.H.P.	Wheel Base	Max. Track	Length	Width	Turning Circle
VANGUARD ...	2,088	4	68	8' 6"	4' 3"	14' 4"	5' 7½"	35'
EIGHT	803	4	28	7'	4' 0½"	11' 10	4' 10"	32'
TEN	948	4	33	7'	4' 0½"	12' 1"	4' 10"	32'
GOOD COMPANION	948	4	33	7'	4' 0½"	12'	4' 10"	32'
2 LITRE ESTATE CAR	2,088¶	4	68	7' 10"	4' 6"	13' 7"	5' 9"	35'

Total U.K. Prices

FAMILY EIGHT	£554 17s.	0d.
SUPER EIGHT (vynide trim)	£608 17s.	0d.
SUPER TEN (vynide trim)..	£646 7s.	0d.
GOOD COMPANION (vynide trim)	£728 17s.	0d.
VANGUARD III (vynide trim)	£899 17s.	0d.
2-LITRE ESTATE CAR (vynide trim)	£950 17s.	0d.

Sunbeam

Sunbeam Talbot Ltd.,
(Rootes Group)

Ryton-on-Dunsmore,

Coventry.

- RAPIER:* 90 m.p.h., 4-cyl., 1·4-litre o.h.v. engine. 4-speed synchromesh gearbox with steering column control. Overdrive. Coil spring and swinging link i.f.s. 2-door, 5-seater hardtop saloon.

- MARK III: 90 m.p.h., 4-cyl., 2¼-litre o.h.v. engine, 4-speed synchromesh gearbox with steering column change. Overdrive optional. Coil spring i.f.s. 4-door, 4-seater saloon.

O NE of the most interesting new cars for 1956 is the Sunbeam Rapier, a 1·4 litre hardtop saloon with a top speed of over 90 m.p.h., and a 30 m.p.g. fuel consumption. The Rapier has overdrive as standard equipment on third and top gears so that in effect it has a six-speed gearbox. It has a full width body with a wide radiator grille of horizontal chromium bars, a curved wind-screen and "wraparound" rear window. The new model is available in two colour combinations, and the inside fittings include a revolution counter, two-speed windscreen wipers and ignition key starting. The engine is basically similar to the Hillman Minx power unit and has a square bore/stroke ratio. The wheels are of typical Sunbeam chromium disc type.

Sunbeam Rapier

Sunbeam Mk III Saloon

The famous Mark III saloon, with its background of rally successes, is continued with only minor changes this year. Like the other Rootes models it is now available in two-tone colour schemes. The 2¼-litre overhead valve engine gives a top speed of about 95 m.p.h., and Laycock de Normanville overdrive is an optional extra. It is a 4-seater sports saloon with a flush-fitting sunshine roof. The Sunbeam radiator is narrow and pointed with a vertical grille and smaller ventilation ports low down on either side.

Specifications

Model	c.c.	No. of Cyls.	Max. B.H.P.	Wheel Base	Max. Track	Length	Width	Turning Circle
RAPIER	1,390	4	62	8'	4' 1"	13' 4"	5'	34' 3"
MARK III	2,267	4	80	8' 1½"	4' 2½"	14'	5' 2½"	36'

Total U.K. Prices

RAPIER   ..   ..   £1,043 17s. 0d.

MARK III   ..   ..   £1,253 17s. 0d.

Triumph

**Triumph Motor Co.
(1945) Ltd.,
Coventry.**

● T.R.3 Sports:* 100 m.p.h.+, 4-cyl., 2-litre, push-rod o.h.v. engine, twin carbs., 4-speed synchromesh gearbox. Optional overdrive. Central change lever. Coil spring and wishbone i.f.s. 2-door, 2-seater, open sports or hard-top.

● T.R.2 Sports: Similar details, but slightly less powerful engine.

THIS year Triumphs are concentrating on a single model, the popular high performance Sports, first introduced as the T.R.2, and now designated the T.R.3. In its new form it has a chromium radiator grille over the oblong radiator orifice and a

Triumph T.R.3 Sports car, showing a close up view of the occasional seat.

power output stepped up from 90 b.h.p. to 95 b.h.p. The 4-cylinder engine is a linered down version of the Vanguard power unit and combined with a total weight of under a ton it gives the T.R.3 a top speed of more than 100 m.p.h. An occasional passenger seat at the rear is now offered as an extra. Another optional extra is a detachable fibre glass hardtop. The wheels are of the drilled disc type, and wire wheels with knock-off hub caps are an extra. Other extras include aero screens and special front springs and rear dampers for competition work. The T.R.2 is still available. The Triumph has already achieved many successes in sports car racing.

Specifications

Model	c.c.	No. of Cyls.	Max. B.H.P.	Wheel Base	Max. Track	Length	Width	Turning Circle
T.R.3	1,991	4	95	7' 4"	3' 9½"	12' 7"	4' 7½"	34
T.R.2	1,991	4	90	7' 4"	3' 9½"	12' 4"	4' 7½"	34'

Total U.K. Prices

T.R.2 Sports	..	..	..	..	..	£938 17s.	0d.
T.R.2 Hardtop	..	..	..	..	..	£1,006 7s.	0d.
T.R.3 Sports	..	..	..	..	..	£976 7s.	0d.
T.R.3 Hardtop	..	..	..	..	..	£1,043 17s.	0d.

Vauxhall

Vauxhall Motors Ltd.,

Luton,

Bedfordshire.

- Wyvern: 70 m.p.h., 4-cyl., 1½-litre " oversquare " o.h.v. engine. 4-speed synchromesh gearbox. Steering column change. Tubeless tyres. 4-door, 4/5-seater saloon.

- Velox: 80 m.p.h., 2¼-litre " over-square " o.h.v. engine. 4-speed synchromesh gearbox. Steering column change. Tubeless tyres. 4-door, 4/5-seater saloon.

- Cresta: De-luxe version of Velox.

THE three popular Vauxhalls, the 4-cylinder Wyvern and 6-cylinder Velox and Cresta models, are continued in 1956 with a number of minor changes. Better visibility is provided by wider windscreens and enlarged rear windows. Wind-up

Vauxhall Velox

windows are fitted instead of the direct lift type. The brakes have been improved and tubeless tyres are standard on all models. There is no longer any need to " run in " a new Vauxhall engine—although the new owner is advised to take things easily for the first 1,000 miles. Note the wide simple grille with its built-in side lamps, and the familiar Vauxhall bonnet flutes. The Wyvern has a petrol consumption of about 35 m.p.g., and the Velox about 30 m.p.g. The de-luxe Cresta model has leather upholstery, white wall tyres, a heater, coat hangers, chromium wheel rim embellishers and various other refinements.

Vauxhall Cresta

Model		c.c.	No. of Cyls.	Max. B.H.P.	Wheel Base	Max. Track	Length	Width	Turning Circle
WYVERN	...	1,507	4	47.5	8' 7"	4' 6½"	14' 2¾"	5' 6½"	38'
VELOX & CRESTA	...	2,262	6	67.5	8' 7"	4' 7¾"	14' 4"	5' 6½"	38'

Total U.K. Prices

WYVERN	..	..	..	..	..	..	£766	7s.	0d.
VELOX	..	..	..	..	..	..	£841	7s.	0d.
CRESTA	..	..	..	..	..	..	£931	7s.	0d.

Wolseley

Wolseley Motors Ltd.,

(Nuffield Organisation)

Cowley,

Oxford.

- FOUR FORTY-FOUR: 80 m.p.h., 1¼-litre, 4-cyl., o.h.v. engine. 4-speed synchromesh gearbox with steering column change. Coil spring and wishbone i.f.s. Fitted heater and demister 4-door, 4-seater saloon.

- SIX NINETY: 90 m.p.h., 2½-litre, 6-cyl., o.h.v. engine. Twin S.U. carbs. 4-speed synchromesh gearbox with steering column change. Torsion bar i.f.s., coil springs at rear. 4-door, 4/5-seater saloon.

EXCEPT that the Six-Eighty has now dropped out, the Wolseley range continues for 1956 without change. The two models are the 4-cylinder, Four Forty-Four saloon, and the 6-cylinder, Six-Ninety saloon. Both have full width bodies, curved one-piece screens, and the typically Wolseley radiator with the illuminated oval nameplate and the narrow upright grille. The Four Forty-Four has coil spring and wishbone independent front suspension and semi-elliptic springs at the rear. The Six-Ninety has independent suspension by torsion bars at the front and coil springs are used at the rear. The 2½-litre engine of the Ninety has twin carburettors. Heater and demister units are fitted as standard equipment on both models.

Total U.K. Prices

FOUR FORTY-FOUR	..	..	..	..	£893	17s.	0d.
SIX NINETY	..	..	..	..	£1,126	7s.	0d.

Wolseley Six Ninety

Specifications

Model			c.c.	No. of Cyls.	Max. B.H.P.	Wheel Base	Max. Track	Length	Width	Turning Circle
4/44	...	...	1,250	4	46	8′ 6″	4′ 3″	14′ 5″	5′ 1″	38′
6/90	...	...	2,639	6	95	9′ 5½″	4′ 6½″	15′ 8″	5′ 7″	37′ 3″

Wolseley Four forty-four

Other *Ian Allan* Books to interest you

AIRCRAFT BOOKS

ABC British Military Aircraft	- 2/6
ABC Civil Aircraft Markings	- 2/6
ABC Civil Aircraft Recognition	- 2/6
ABC Helicopters - - -	- 2/6
ABC U.S. and Canadian Aircraft	- 2/6
ABC Continental Military Aircraft	2/6

SHIP BOOKS

ABC Ocean Liners - -	- 2/6
ABC Ocean Freighters - -	- 2/6
ABC Ocean Tankers - -	- 2/6
ABC Coastal Steamers - -	- 2/6
ABC British Railways Steamers	- 2/-
British Canals - -	- 3/6
Steamers of the Solent -	- 2/6